TSW Publishing
P. O. Box 176
Centreville, Virginia 20122
www.scholarshipworkshop.com
TSW Publishing is a division of The Scholarship Workshop LLC

The Scholarship Monthly Planner was written to provide accurate advice to readers. However, please note that the author nor the publisher are engaged in the practice of providing legal, accounting, tax or other professional advice. If you need legal, accounting, tax or other advice, please consult a professional in the appropriate area. Neither the author, the publisher, nor any entity associated with The Scholarship Monthly Planner assume any liability for errors, omissions, or inaccuracies. Any action you take or do not take as a result of reading The Scholarship Monthly Planner is entirely your responsibility.

ISBN: 978-1-950653-16-4

Printed in the United States of America

This resource is available at special quantity discounts for bulk purchases for sales promotions, premiums, fundraising, and educational use. Special versions or excerpts can also be created to fit specific needs.

The Scholarship Monthly Planner
2021-2022

The Scholarship Monthly Planner

August 2021

*Programs are open to current college students and high school seniors.

**Programs are open to current college students only.

***Programs are open to graduate and/or professional school students only.

+Program open to graduate and undergraduate students

Unless otherwise noted, all other programs are open to high school seniors.

SUN	MON	TUE	WED	THU	FRI	SAT
When visiting web-sites, you may need to use the search box on the site or scroll through the home page to find the specific scholarship program listed.		Look at all deadlines for upcoming scholarships you've already re-searched. Be sure they are included in your calendar.		Work on your scholarship résumé/activity list.		Check website for VFW Voice of De-mocracy Audio Essay Contest rules — https://www.vfw.org/community/youth-and-education/youth-scholarships
1 **Chuan Ai Lu Engstrom Memorial Scholarship deadline — https://pcb-solutions.com/scholarship/	2 *Begin working on Ayn Rand "Atlas Shrugged" Essay Contest entry — https://www.aynrand.org/students/essay-contests# ——— Check website for application: Coca-Cola Scholars Foundation — www.coca-colascholarsfoundation.org	3 *Check website for VFW Patriot's Pen Essay Contest rules — https://www.vfw.org/community/youth-and-education/youth-scholarships	4 Check website for Horatio Alger National Scholarship Application — www.horatioalger.org or https://scholars.horatioalger.org ——— Check website for Gates Scholarship Application — https://www.thegatesscholarship.org/scholarship	5 Check website for Regeneron Science Talent Search process and rules — https://student.societyforscience.org/regeneron-sts ——— Check website for United States Senate Youth Program application process and regional deadlines — http://ussenateyouth.org	6 Check website for National YoungArts Foundation competi-tion entry rules — www.youngarts.org ——— **Check website for Scholarship America Dream Award Appli-cation — https://scholarshipameri-ca.org/students/browse-scholarships/apply-for-the-dream-award	7 *Check website for Bonsai Finance Veteran's Scholar-ship - https://bonsaifinance.com/veterans-scholarship/ ——— Contact your local American Legion chapter for infor-mation on The Ameri-can Legion National High School Oratori-cal Contest — www.legion.org
8 Check website for Dr. Pepper Tuition Giveaway entry rules— www.drpeppertuition.com or (OPEN TO STUDENTS 18 YEARS AND OLDER)	9 **Check website for Student Loan Hero $5K Scholarship—https://studentloanhero.com/scholarships/	10 Check website for Prudential Spirit of Community Award process — http://spirit.prudential.com/view/page/soc/301 (OPEN TO STUDENTS IN GRADES 5 THRU 12)	11 Check website for Davidson Fellows Scholarship application process — http://www.davidsongifted.org/Fellows-Scholarship (OPEN TO ALL STUDENTS UNDER AGE 18)	12 Check website for Cameron Impact Scholar-ship — https://www.bryancameroneducationfoundation.org	13 Check website for QuestBridge National College Match appli-cation process — www.questbridge.org ——— Also see www.facebook.com/questbridge or https://twitter.com/questbridge	14 +Check website for The Christophers Annual Video Contest — https://www.christophers.org or https://www.christophers.org/video-contest-for-college-students
15 Check website for the Anne Ford Scholar-ship application — www.ncld.org ——— Check with your stu-dent chapter advisor: DECA Scholarship Program — www.deca.org/scholarships	16 ***Check website for Beinecke Scholar-ship nomination pro-cess — http://fdnweb.org/beinecke ——— **Check website for Adobe Research Women-in-Technology Scholarship applica-tion— https://research.adobe.com/scholarship	17 **DO THIS NOW!** Review scholarship résumé/activity list for areas to improve such as community service, leadership, overall involvement. A well-rounded student has a better chance of win-ning scholarships.	18 Check website for entry kit: Toshiba NSTA ExploraVision Awards — www.exploravision.org (OPEN TO STUDENTS IN GRADES K—12)	19 Check website for Soroptimist Live Your Dream Awards — https://www.soroptimist.org/our-work/live-your-dream-awards (OPEN TO WOMEN WHO ARE PRIMARY FINANICIAL SUPPORT FOR THEIR HOUSEHOLD)	20 Check website Don't Text and Drive Scholarship entry rules — www.digitalresponsibility.org/dont-text-and-drive-scholarship/	21 **Check for NASA Scholarship and Fellowship Opportunities — https://intern.nasa.gov or https://www.nasa.gov/stem/fellowships-scholarships
22 **Check website for Scholarship Ameri-ca Dream Award Application — https://scholarshipameri-ca.org/students/browse-scholarships/apply-for-the-dream-award	23 +Check website for application: SMART Scholarship Program — https://www.smartscholarship.org/smart	24 Check website for Gates Scholarship Application — https://www.thegatesscholarship.org	25 Check website for entry rules: American Fire Sprinkler Associa-tion Second Chance Scholarship Contest — www.afsascholarship.org FOR NONTRADITION-AL STUDENTS Also see @afsascholarship or www.facebook.com/afsascholarship/	26 If you are a junior, start preparing for the PSAT which may be given by your high school in October.	27 Contact the National Society of the Daughters of the American Revolution (NSDAR) for infor-mation about their scholarship programs — www.dar.org or https://dar.academicworks.com	28 Contact your local American Legion chapter for infor-mation on The Ameri-can Legion National High School Oratori-cal Contest — www.legion.org
29 Check website for Hispanic Heritage Youth Awards applica-tion — https://hhfawards.hispanicheritage.org/2021	30 **Check website for Optimal Scholar-ships — https://www.optimal.com/scholarships	31				

The Scholarship Monthly Planner

Notes

The Scholarship Monthly Planner

September 2021

Notes (left margin):

*Programs are open to current college students and high school seniors.

**Programs are open to current college students only.

***Programs are open to graduate and/or professional school students only.

+Program open to graduate and undergraduate students

Unless otherwise noted, all other programs are open to high school seniors.

SUN	MON	TUE	WED	THU	FRI	SAT
When visiting websites, you may need to use the search box on the site or scroll through the home page to find the specific scholarship program listed. *To get alerts of upcoming deadlines and new scholarship opportunities, like The Scholarship Workshop on Facebook, follow us @ScholarshipWork on Twitter and Instagram.com/scholarshipworkshop.* *You can also text SCHOLARSHIPINFO to 22828 to join our mailing list for updates!*						Check website for National Beta Club scholarship application — www.betaclub.org/scholarship
Check website for application: Elks Most Valuable Student Contest — www.elks.org/enf/scholars/mvs.cfm or contact your local Elks lodge	Check website for application process and regional deadline: Junior Science and Humanities Symposium (JSHS) Program — www.jshs.org (OPEN TO GRADES 9 THRU 12)	Check website for application: Equitable Excellence Scholarship— https://equitable.com/foundation/equitable-excellence-scholarship	**1** American Fire Sprinkler Association Second Chance Scholarship Contest entry due — www.afsascholarship.org FOR NONTRADITIONAL STUDENTS Also see @afsascholarship or www.facebook.com/afsascholarship/	**2** Check website for Ron Brown Scholarship application — www.ronbrown.org	**3** ***Check website for GEM fellowship application— www.gemfellowship.org	**4** Check website for rules: American Fire Sprinkler Association High School Senior Scholarship Contest — www.afsascholarship.org
5 **Check website for Jack Kent Cooke Undergraduate Transfer Scholarship application — www.jkcf.org	**6** **Check website for Scholarship America Dream Award Application — https://scholarshipamerica.org/students/browse-scholarships/apply-for-the-dream-award	**7** Check website for Jack Kent Cooke College Scholarship Program application — www.jkcf.org	**8** **Contact dean's office or department chair for nomination process: Coca-Cola Community College Academic Team Scholarship — www.ptk.org (See Scholarships)	**9** Check website for application: Scholastic Art and Writing Awards — www.artandwriting.org (OPEN TO GRADES 7 THRU 12)	**10** Cameron Impact Scholarship application due — https://www.bryancameroneducationfoundation.org	**11** Check website for The Christophers Annual Poster Contest — https://www.christophers.org or https://www.christophers.org/poster-contest (OPEN TO STUDENTS IN GRADES 9 THRU 12)
12 **Check website for Coupons Plus Deals Scholarship— https://www.couponsplusdeals.com/scholarship (OPEN TO 3RD OR 4TH YEAR COLLEGE STUDENTS)	**13** Check website for Mu Alpha Theta Kalin Award nomination process—https://mualphatheta.org/kalin_award	**14** Check website: Dr. Arnita Young Boswell Scholarship — www.nhbwinc.com or https://nhbwinc.com/scholarships	**15** Gates Scholarship Application due — https://www.thegatesscholarship.org	**16** Check website for Jack Kent Cooke College Scholarship Program application — www.jkcf.org	**17** Check website for C-Span's StudentCam competition — http://www.studentcam.org (OPEN TO STUDENTS IN GRADES 6 THRU 12)	**18** *Check website for HOTH SEO Scholarship Program—https://www.thehoth.com/seo-scholarship
19 Check website for entry kit: Toshiba NSTA ExploraVision Awards — www.exploravision.org (OPEN TO STUDENTS IN GRADES K—12)	**20** Check website for National Security Agency Stokes Educational Scholarship Program application — www.intelligencecareers.gov/icstudents.html	**21** Check out College Board Opportunity Scholarships — https://opportunity.collegeboard.org/home	**22** *Check website for Create-A-Greeting-Card Scholarship Contest entry rules — www.gallerycollection.com/greetingcardscontests.htm (OPEN TO NONTRADITIONAL STUDENTS)	**23** Check website for John F. Kennedy Profile in Courage Essay Contest rules — www.jfklibrary.org (OPEN TO GRADES 9 THRU 12)	**24** **Adobe Research Women-in-Technology Scholarship application due soon — https://research.adobe.com/	**25**
26 Consider applying early for the Equitable Excellence Scholarship *(there may be an application limit)*— https://equitable.com/foundation/equitable-excellence-scholarship	**27** Ayn Rand "Atlas Shrugged" Essay Contest entry due — https://www.aynrand.org/students/essay-contests#	**28** QuestBridge National College Match application due — www.questbridge.org Also see www.facebook.com/questbridge or https://twitter.com/questbridge	**29** Don't Text and Drive Scholarship deadline SEPTEMBER 30 — www.digitalresponsibility.org/dont-text-and-drive-scholarship/ ——— **Optimal Scholarships application due SEPTEMBER 30 — https://www.optimal.com/scholarships/	**30** *Bonsai Finance Veteran's Scholarship Application due - https://bonsaifinance.com/veterans-scholarship		

The Scholarship Monthly Planner

Notes

_____

_____

_____

_____

_____

_____

_____

_____

_____

_____

_____

_____

_____

_____

_____

_____

_____

_____

_____

_____

_____

_____

_____

DON'T FORGET!

- Final deadline dates have red text.
- Submit your application at least 7 days before the deadline.
- Always look at least 1 month ahead to get prepared for upcoming deadlines.
- Hate writing? Start on your essay at least 1 month prior to the deadline.
- Need recommendations? Ask at least 4 weeks prior to the deadline. Follow-up! Also, many programs request recommendations electronically. Please let someone know you've provided their e-mail address for a recommendation, so they will be prepared for the e-mail request.
- As you download applications, organize them. You should have one folder for each month. Place applications in the appropriate folder for each month. For example, all applications that are due in December should be in a folder marked December.
- Check previous months for application download dates or activities you need to complete. These activities are shown in black text. Although you may be behind with some activities, the deadline date for a scholarship or award may not have passed.
- Research and include local, regional, and state based scholarships in your calendar.
- Research and include scholarships based on your interests, personal characteristics, and situation in your calendar.
- Request nominations with a letter and your résumé.

The Scholarship Monthly Planner
October 2021

*Programs are open to current college students and high school seniors.

**Programs are open to current college students only.

***Programs are open to graduate and/or professional school students only.

+Program open to graduate and undergraduate students

Unless otherwise noted, all other programs are open to high school seniors.

SUN	MON	TUE	WED	THU	FRI	SAT
				If you are a high school junior, get ready to take the PSAT this month. Scoring well among students in your state could qualify you for a National Merit scholarship.	**1** ***GEM fellowship application for early consideration due OCTOBER 1 (Supplemental Materials must be in by Final Deadline of November 15) — www.gemfellowship.org	**2** Contact your local Optimist Club for information about the Optimist International Essay and Oratorical Contests — www.optimist.org (OPEN TO STUDENTS UNDER AGE 19)
3 +Check website for American Association on Health & Disability Scholarship Program—https://www.aahd.us/initiatives/scholarship-program/ (OPEN TO STUDENTS WITH DISABILITIES) *Note: This scholarship may be suspended due to COVID.-19*	**4** **Student Loan Hero $5K Scholarship application due —https://studentloanhero.com/scholarships/	**5** Contact the National Society of the Daughters of the American Revolution (NSDAR) for information about their scholarship programs — www.dar.org or https://dar.academicworks.com	**6** Start working on your Free application for Federal Student Aid (FAFSA) — www.fafsa.ed.gov or https://studentaid.gov/h/apply-for-aid/fafsa Also contact schools and states for their specific deadlines.	**7** ***Contact your medical school's dean, student affairs or financial aid office to be considered for an AMA Foundation scholarship nomination — https://amafoundation.org/programs/scholarships/ or https://amaf.smapply.io/	**8**	**9** Check website: Stop Hunger Scholarship Program application and deadline — www.sodexofoundation.org or http://us.stop-hunger.org/home/grants.html
10 Check website for The Google Lime Scholarship —https://edu.google.com/scholarships/the-google-lime-scholarship/ (OPEN TO STUDENTS WITH DISABILITIES)	**11** **Check website for CC Bank's Young Scholars Scholarship application — https://ccbank.us/scholarship/	**12** Check website for Dell Scholarship Program application — www.dellscholars.org	**13** Get sponsor for — www.fra.org (see Events and Program < Americanism Essay Contest) (OPEN TO GRADES 7 THRU 12) Deadline for sponsored entries December 1.	**14** Hispanic Heritage Youth Awards application due — https://hhfawards.hispanicheritage.org/2021	**15** National YoungArts Foundation competition entry due — www.youngarts.org **Scholarship America Dream Award Application due—https://learn-more.scholarsapply.org/dreamaward/	**16**
17 **Dr. Pepper Tuition Giveaway entry due — www.drpeppertuition.com (OPEN TO STUDENTS 18 YEARS AND OLDER)	**18** Are you a female currently studying engineering, engineering technology and computer science ? If yes, visit this page for many opportunities through the Society of Women Engineers — https://swe.org/scholarships/ or www.swe.org (see Scholarships)	**19** *Have a disability? Check website for Wells Fargo Scholarship Program for People with Disabilities — https://learn-more.scholarsapply.org/pwdscholarship/ Apply early or NOW. They have a strict application limit.	**20** Check website for Foot Locker Scholar Athletes Scholarship application — https://footlockerscholarathletes.com/	**21** Check website for application: Burger King Scholars Program — www.bkmclamorefoundation.org or https://burgerking.scholarsapply.org	**22** Check out College Board Opportunity Scholarships — https://opportunity.collegeboard.org/home	**23** Check website for entry rules: "Frame My Future" Scholarship Contest — www.framemyfuture.com or https://www.diplomaframe.com/contests/frame-my-future-scholarship.aspx
24 **Check website for nomination process — All-USA Community College Academic Team — www.ptk.org (see Scholarships)	**25** Check out the Horatio Alger Scholarship Application — www.horatioalger.org or https://scholars.horatioalger.org	**26**	**27** *2021 Overcoming Obstacles Scholarship application due OCTOBER 31 — 2021 Overcoming Obstacles Scholarship - Whitley Law Firm — https://whitleylawfirm.com/2021-overcoming-obstacles-scholarship/	**28** National Security Agency Stokes Educational Scholarship Program application due OCTOBER 31 — www.intelligencecareers.gov/icstudents.html	**29** VFW Voice of Democracy Audio Essay Contest deadline—OCTOBER 31 — https://www.vfw.org/community/youth-and-education/youth-scholarships (OPEN TO GRADES 9 THRU 12)	**30** VFW Patriot's Pen Essay Contest entries due OCTOBER 31— https://www.vfw.org/community/youth-and-education/youth-scholarships (OPEN TO GRADES 6 THRU 8)
31 Coca-Cola Scholarship application due — www.coca-colascholarsfoundation.org/						

The Scholarship Monthly Planner

Notes

The Scholarship Monthly Planner
November 2021

*Programs are open to current college students and high school seniors.

**Programs are open to current college students only.

***Programs are open to graduate and/or professional school students only.

+Program open to graduate and undergraduate students

Unless otherwise noted, all other programs are open to high school seniors.

SUN	MON	TUE	WED	THU	FRI	SAT
	1 Ron Brown Scholarship application due (early application deadline) — www.ronbrown.org	**2** Prudential Spirit of Community Awards application due soon — http://spirit.prudential.com/view/page/soc/301 (OPEN TO STUDENTS IN GRADES 5 THRU 12)	**3** Anne Ford Scholarship application due soon — www.ncld.org (OPEN TO STUDENTS WITH LEARNING DISABILITIES) Allegra Ford Thomas Scholarship application due soon— www.ncld.org (OPEN TO STUDENTS WITH LEARNING DISABILITIES)	**4** Contact your National Honor Society advisor to be considered for a NHS Scholarship program nomination — www.nhs.us/scholarship	**5** **Check website for RISE Financial Progress Scholarship application — https://www.risecredit.com/rise-scholarship	**6** Check website for Amazon Future Engineer Scholarship — https://learn-more.scholarsapply.org/amazonfutureengineer/
7 Check website for Stockholm Junior Water Prize state competition entry forms — www.wef.org/SJWP/ (OPEN TO GRADES 9 THRU 12)	**8** Check website for Dell Scholarship Program application — www.dellscholars.org	**9** **Check website for Coupons Plus Deals Scholarship—https://www.couponsplusdeals.com/scholarship (OPEN TO 3RD OR 4TH YEAR COLLEGE STUDENTS)	**10** Regeneron Science Talent Search entry due — www.societyforscience.org/sts or student.societyforscience.org/regeneron-sts	**11** +Check website for Alpha Kappa Alpha Educational Advancement Scholarship application — www.akaeaf.org	**12** Check website for application: Jackie Robinson Scholarship Program — www.jackierobinson.org	**13** Soroptimist Live Your Dream Awards application due NOVEMBER 15— https://www.soroptimist.org/our-work/live-your-dream-awards (OPEN TO WOMEN WHO ARE PRIMARY FINANCIAL SUPPORT FOR THEIR HOUSEHOLD)
14 Check website for application: DEWALT Trades Scholarship — https://learn-more.scholarsapply.org/dewalttrade/ (OPEN TO STUDENTS ATTENDING TWO-YEAR COLLEGE OR VOCATIONAL-TECHNICAL SCHOOLS)	**15** Elks Most Valuable Student application due — www.elks.org/enf/scholars/ ***GEM fellowship application due— www.gemfellowship.org	**16** ***Contact your medical school's dean, student affairs or financial aid office to be considered for an AMA Foundation Physicians of Tomorrow Scholarship nomination —https://amafoundation.org/programs/scholarships/ or https://amaf.smapply.io/	**17** Check website for GE–Reagan Foundation Scholarship Program application — www.reaganfoundation.org/ge-rfscholarships.aspx Also see https://www.facebook.com/GEReaganScholarships	**18** Jack Kent Cooke College Scholarship Program application due —https://www.jkcf.org/our-scholarships/young-scholars-program/	**19** *Check website for Create-A-Greeting-Card Scholarship Contest entry rules — www.gallerycollection.com/greetingcardscontests.htm (OPEN TO NONTRADITIONAL STUDENTS)	**20** *Check website for Taco Bell Live Mas Scholarship — https://www.tacobellfoundation.org/live-mas-scholarship/
21 If you're in NHS, contact your school for their National Honor Society Scholarship Program nomination deadline — www.nhs.us/scholarship	**22** **Check website for Chuan Ai Lu Engstrom Memorial Spring Scholarship entry rules—https://pcb-solutions.com/scholarship/	**23** Check website for application: Jeanette Rankin Women's Scholarship — www.rankinfoundation.org (OPEN TO WOMEN 35+)	**24** Check out College Board Opportunity Scholarships — https://opportunity.collegeboard.org/home	**25**	**26** Check website for Military Commanders' Scholarship application - https://learn-more.scholarsapply.org/militarycommanders/	**27** **Check website for Ritchie-Jennings Memorial Scholarship application — www.acfe.com/scholarship.aspx
28	**29** If you haven't already, start working on your Free application for Federal Student Aid (FAFSA) — www.fafsa.ed.gov Also contact schools and states for their specific deadlines.	**30** Check website: American Foreign Service Essay Contest entry rules —www.afsa.org/essaycontest/				

The Scholarship Monthly Planner

Notes

The Scholarship Monthly Planner
December 2021

*Programs are open to current college students **and** high school seniors.

**Programs are open to current college students only.

***Programs are open to graduate and/or professional school students only.

+Program open to graduate and undergraduate students

Unless otherwise noted, all other programs are open to high school seniors.

SUN	MON	TUE	WED	THU	FRI	SAT
**Chuan Ai Lu Engstrom Memorial Spring Scholarship deadline DECEMBER 1 — https://pcb-solutions.com/scholarship/	Americanism Essay Contest entries due DECEMBER 1 — www.fra.org (see Events and Program < Americanism Essay Contest) (OPEN TO GRADES 7 THRU 12)	Dell Scholarship Program application due DECEMBER 1 — www.dellscholars.org	**1** +SMART Scholarship Program application due — https://smartscholarship-prod.service-now.com/smart **Application due for Coca-Cola Community College Academic Team www.ptk.org (*see Scholarships*)	**2** Google Lime Scholarship deadline soon — https://www.limeconnect.com/programs/page/google-lime-scholarship (OPEN TO STUDENTS WITH DISABILITIES)	**3** +The Christophers Annual Video Contest entry due soon — https://www.christophers.org or https://www.christophers.org/video-contest-for-college-students	**4**
5 +*Stop Hunger Scholarship Program deadline — www.sodexofoundation.org or http://us.stop-hunger.org/home/grants.html (OPEN TO STUDENTS IN KINDERGARTEN THROUGH GRADUATE SCHOOL)	**6**	**7**	**8**	**9** Contact your local Executive Women International chapter for information on Adult Students in Scholastic Transition scholarship nomination process — www.ewiconnect.com (OPEN TO ADULT STUDENTS)	**10** Equitable Excellence Scholarship application due soon (*there may be an application limit so apply early*) — https://equitable.com/foundation/equitable-excellence-scholarship	**11** *Check website for application: Hispanic Scholarship Fund — www.hsf.net
12 Optimist International Essay and Oratorical Contests deadline in late December (contact local club for specific dates) — www.optimist.org/e/member/scholarships1.cfm# (OPEN TO STUDENTS UNDER AGE 19 AS OF 10/1/2021)	**13** DEWALT Trades Scholarship application due — https://learn-more.scholarsapply.org/dewalttrade/ (OPEN TO STUDENTS ATTENDING TWO-YEAR COLLEGE OR VOCATIONAL-TECHNICAL SCHOOL)S	**14** Foot Locker Scholar Athletes Scholarship application due soon — https://footlockerscholarathletes.com	**15** Burger King Scholars Program application due — www.bkmclamorefoundation.org or burgerking.scholarsapply.org	**16** Check website for The George S. & Stella M. Knight Essay Contest information and rules — www.sar.org (see Education) (OPEN TO GRADES 10 THRU 12)	**17** Check website for Mu Alpha Theta Scholarships — www.mualphatheta.org	**18** Check website for application: Scholarships for Military Children — www.militaryscholar.org or https://fisherhouse.org/programs/scholarship-programs
19 Check website for The Joseph S. Rumbaugh Historical Oration Contest information and rules — www.sar.org (Education)	**20** Check website for DECA Scholarship Program application — www.deca.org/scholarships	**21**	**22** Use the FAFSA4caster to get an early estimate of your eligibility for federal student aid — https://fafsa.ed.gov/spa/fafsa4c	**23** Check website for Doodle 4 Google entry rules — www.google.com/doodle4google (OPEN TO STUDENTS IN KINDERGARTEN THRU 12)	**24**	**25** Check website for Simon Youth Foundation Scholarship application — https://syf.org/scholarships/ Also see https://www.facebook.com/simonyouthfoundation or https://twitter.com/simon_youth
26 Check out College Board Opportunity Scholarships — https://opportunity.collegeboard.org/home	**27** +Check website for application: Military Spouse Scholarships — https://www.militaryfamily.org/programs/spouses-scholarships/ (OPEN TO NONTRADITIONAL STUDENTS)	**28**	**29** CC Bank's Young Scholars Scholarship application due DECEMBER 31 — https://ccbank.us/scholarship	**30** *HOTH SEO Scholarship Program deadline DECEMBER 31 — https://www.thehoth.com/seo-scholarship	**31** **Deadline for Coupons Plus Deals Scholarship — https://www.couponsplusdeals.com/scholarship (OPEN TO 3RD OR 4TH YEAR COLLEGE STUDENTS, ALSO OPEN TO INTERNATIONAL STUDENTS)	

The Scholarship Monthly Planner

Notes

The Scholarship Monthly Planner
January 2022

*Programs are open to current college students and high school seniors.

**Programs are open to current college students only.

***Programs are open to graduate and/or professional school students only.

+Program open to graduate and undergraduate students

Unless otherwise noted, all other programs are open to high school seniors.

SUN	MON	TUE	WED	THU	FRI	SAT
				Contact the National Society of the Daughters of the American Revolution (NSDAR) for information about their scholarship programs — www.dar.org or https://dar.academicworks.com	Taco Bell Live Mas Scholarship deadline this month — https://www.tacobellfoundation.org/live-mas-scholarship/	**1** **Check for NASA Scholarship and Fellowship Opportunities — https://intern.nasa.gov or https://www.nasa.gov/stem/fellowships-scholarships
2 Check website for application: Jeanette Rankin Women's Scholarship — www.rankinfoundation.org (OPEN TO WOMEN 35+)	**3** Check website for Mu Alpha Theta Scholarships — www.mualphatheta.org*	**4** Contact your local Executive Women International chapter for information on EWISP scholarship nomination process — www.ewiconnect.com	**5** **Check website for Wells Fargo Veterans Scholarship program application - https://learn-more.scholarsapply.org/wellsfargoveterans/	**6** *Check website for Orphan Foundation of America Foster Care to Success scholarship application — http://fc2success.org/	**7** Check website for application: Hispanic Scholarship Fund — www.hsf.net	**8** GE–Reagan Foundation Scholarship Program application deadline JANUARY 10 — www.reaganfoundation.org/ge-rfscholarships.aspx or https://www.facebook.com/GEReaganScholarships
9 Ron Brown Scholar application due (Final Postmark Deadline) - www.ronbrown.org	**10** **Jack Kent Cooke Undergraduate Transfer Scholarship application due — www.jkcf.org	**11** Check website for Jack Kent Cooke Young Scholars Program application — https://www.jkcf.org/our-scholarships/young-scholars-program/ (OPEN TO 7TH GRADE STUDENTS ONLY)	**12** *Check website for 100 Black Men Scholarship — www.100blackmen.org, https://100blackmen.org/program-activations/annual-scholarship-program or contact a local chapter	**13** Check website for Gloria Barron Prize for Young Heroes application — https://barronprize.org/apply (OPEN TO STUDENTS AGE 8 TO 18)	**14** DECA Scholarship Program application due — www.deca.org/scholarships — John F. Kennedy Profile in Courage Essay Contest entry due soon — www.jfklibrary.org/ (OPEN TO GRADES 9 THRU 12)	**15** If you haven't already, start working on your Free application for Federal Student Aid (FAFSA) — www.fafsa.ed.gov or https://studentaid.gov/ Contact schools and states for their specific deadlines.
16 Check website for Doodle 4 Google entry rules and deadline — www.google.com/doodle4google (OPEN TO STUDENTS IN KINDERGARTEN THRU 12)	**17** *Check website for Lockheed Martin STEM Scholarship application — www.lockheedmartin.com/scholarship	**18** Check out College Board Opportunity Scholarships — https://opportunity.collegeboard.org/home	**19** National Beta Club scholarship application due soon — www.betaclub.org/scholarship	**20** C-Span's StudentCam competition deadline — http://www.studentcam.org (OPEN TO STUDENTS IN GRADES 6 THRU 12)	**21** Check website for Lockheed Martin Vocational Scholarship application — https://lockheedmartin.com/en-us/who-we-are/communities/stem-education/lockheed-martin-vocational-scholarship.html	**22**
23 Check website: Dr. Arnita Young Boswell Scholarship — www.nhbwinc.com or https://nhbwinc.org/scholarships	**24** *+Check website for OppU Achievers Scholarship — https://www.opploans.com/scholarship	**25**	**26** *+Check website for Dr. Angela E. Grant Memorial Scholarship deadline — http://drangelagrantscholarship.org (OPEN TO CANCER SURVIVORS OR THOSE WITH IMMEDIATE FAMILY MEMBERS DIAGNOSED WITH CANCER)	**27** Check website for Sweet and Simple Scholarship — https://www.unigo.com/scholarships/our-scholarships/sweet-and-simple-scholarship (OPEN TO STUDENTS AGE 13 AND UP)	**28**	**29**
30	**31** National Society of the Daughters of the American Revolution (NSDAR) scholarship application due — www.dar.org or https://dar.academicworks.com					

The Scholarship Monthly Planner

Notes

_____
_____
_____
_____
_____
_____
_____
_____
_____
_____
_____
_____
_____
_____
_____
_____
_____
_____
_____
_____
_____
_____
_____
_____
_____
_____
_____

DON'T FORGET!

- Final deadline dates have red text.
- Submit your application at least 7 days before the deadline.
- Always look at least 1 month ahead to get prepared for upcoming deadlines.
- Hate writing? Start on your essay at least 1 month prior to the deadline.
- Need recommendations? Ask at least 4 weeks prior to the deadline. Follow-up! Also, many programs request recommendations electronically. Please let someone know you've provided their e-mail address for a recommendation, so they will be prepared for the e-mail request.
- As you download applications, organize You should have for each month cations in For folder tons example ber that shs for

The Scholarship Monthly Planner
February 2022

*Programs are open to current college students and high school seniors.

**Programs are open to current college students only.

***Programs are open to graduate and/or professional school students only.

+P? open to ? and ?uate

SUN	MON	TUE	WED	THU	FRI	SAT
*+Hispanic Scholarship Fund application due this month — www.hsf.net	*Mu Alpha Theta Scholarship application due FEBRUARY 1— www.mualphatheta.org	**1** Jackie Robinson scholarship application due — www.jackierobinson.org	**2** Check website: Life Lessons Essay and Video Contest — www.lifehappens.org/life-lessons (FOR STUDENTS WHO HAVE BEEN AFFECTED BY THE DEATH OF A PARENT OR GUARDIAN)	**3** The Christophers Annual Poster Contest deadline this month — https://www.christophers.org or https://www.christophers.org/poster-contest	**4** **Ritchie-Jennings Memorial Scholarship application due — www.acfe.com/scholarship.aspx	**5** Check website for BHW Women in STEM Scholarship application—https://thebhwgroup.com/scholarship (ALSO OPEN TO INTERNATIONAL STUDENTS)
6	**7** Begin working on Ayn Rand "Anthem" Essay Contest entry or www.aynrand.org/students/essay-contests — www.aynrand.org (OPEN TO GRADES 8 THRU 12)	**8** Check website for Henkel Diversity Scholarship application — https://learn-more.scholarsapply.org/henkeldiversity/	**9** Entry due for Davidson Fellows Scholarship application process — http://www.davidsongifted.org/Fellows-Scholarship (OPEN TO ALL STUDENTS UNDER AGE 18) — — — ***Deadline for Beinecke Scholarship nomination — http://fdnweb.org/beinecke/	**10** +Check website for International Bridge, Tunnel and Turnpike Association Scholarship Program application — https://www.ibtta.org/ibtta-foundation-scholarship-program	**11**	**12** Check website for Horatio Alger Career & Technical Scholarship Program Application — www.horatioalger.org or https://scholars.horatioalger.org
13 Simon Youth Foundation Scholarship application due soon — https://syf.org/scholarships/ Also see https://www.facebook.com/simonyouthfoundation or https://twitter.com/simon_youth	**14** Toshiba NSTA ExploraVision Awards application due this month — www.exploravision.org (OPEN TO STUDENTS IN GRADES K—12)	**15** Doodle 4 Google entry due soon — www.google.com/doodle4google (OPEN TO STUDENTS IN KINDERGARTEN THRU 12)	**16** Jeanette Rankin Women's Scholarship Fund application due soon — www.rankinfoundation.org (OPEN TO WOMEN 35 AND UP)	**17** Amazon Future Engineer Scholarship application due — https://learn-more.scholarsapply.org/amazonfutureengineer/	**18** Scholarships for Military Children application due — https://militaryscholar.org or https://fisherhouse.org/programs/scholarship-programs	**19** *Check website for Central Intelligence Agency (CIA) Undergraduate Scholarship Program application — https://www.cia.gov/careers/jobs/undergraduate-scholarship-program/
20 ***Check website for Central Intelligence Agency (CIA) Graduate Studies Scholarship Program application — https://www.cia.gov/careers/jobs/graduate-scholarship-program/	**21** **Check website—National Association for Campus Activities for scholarship opportunities - https://www.naca.org/FOUNDATION/Pages/Scholarships.aspx	**22** *+Check website for OppU Achievers Scholarship — https://www.opploans.com/scholarship	**23** Check website for Super Power Scholarship — https://www.unigo.com/scholarships/our-scholarships/superpower-scholarship (OPEN TO STUDENTS AGE 13 AND UP)	**24** *Check website for Bristol-Myers Squibb Scholarship for Cancer Survivors — https://learn-more.scholarsapply.org/cancer-survivors/ (OPEN TO STUDENTS 25 YEARS OLD OR YOUNGER)	**25**	**26**
and Simple application ?RY 28 — ?nigo.com/ ?et-and ?ip ?ENTS	**28** Life Lessons Essay and Video Contest application due MARCH 1 — www.lifehappens.org/life-lessons (FOR STUDENTS WHO HAVE BEEN AFFECTED BY THE DEATH OF A PARENT OR GUARDIAN)					

The Scholarship Monthly Planner

Notes

_____
_____
_____
_____
_____
_____
_____
_____
_____
_____
_____
_____
_____
_____
_____
_____
_____
_____
_____
_____
_____
_____
_____
_____
_____

DON'T FORGET!

- Final deadline dates have red text.
- Submit your application at least 7 days before the deadline.
- Always look at least 1 month ahead to get prepared for upcoming deadlines.
- Hate writing? Start on your essay at least 1 month prior to the deadline.
- Need recommendations? Ask at least 4 weeks prior to the deadline. Follow-up! Also, many programs request recommendations electronically. Please let someone know you've provided their e-mail address for a recommendation, so they will be prepared for the e-mail request.
- As you download applications, organize them. You should have one folder for each month. Place applications in the appropriate folder for each month. For example, all applications that are due in December should be in a folder marked December.
- Check previous months for application download dates or activities you need to complete. These activities are shown in black text. Although you may be behind with some activities, the deadline date for a scholarship or award may not have passed.
- Research and include local, regional, and state based scholarships in your calendar.
- Research and include scholarships based on your interests, personal characteristics, and situation in your calendar.
- Request nominations with a letter and your résumé.

The Scholarship Monthly Planner
February 2022

Legend (left margin):

*Programs are open to current college students and high school seniors.

**Programs are open to current college students only.

***Programs are open to graduate and/or professional school students only.

+Program open to graduate and undergraduate students

Unless otherwise noted, all other programs are open to high school seniors.

SUN	MON	TUE	WED	THU	FRI	SAT
*+Hispanic Scholarship Fund application due this month — www.hsf.net	*Mu Alpha Theta Scholarship application due FEBRUARY 1— www.mualphatheta.org	**1** Jackie Robinson scholarship application due — www.jackierobinson.org	**2** Check website: Life Lessons Essay and Video Contest — www.lifehappens.org/life-lessons (FOR STUDENTS WHO HAVE BEEN AFFECTED BY THE DEATH OF A PARENT OR GUARDIAN)	**3** The Christophers Annual Poster Contest deadline this month — https://www.christophers.org or https://www.christophers.org/poster-contest	**4** **Ritchie-Jennings Memorial Scholarship application due — www.acfe.com/scholarship.aspx	**5** Check website for BHW Women in STEM Scholarship application—https://thebhwgroup.com/scholarship (ALSO OPEN TO INTERNATIONAL STUDENTS)
6	**7** Begin working on Ayn Rand "Anthem" Essay Contest entry or www.aynrand.org/students/essay-contests — www.aynrand.org (OPEN TO GRADES 8 THRU 12)	**8** Check website for Henkel Diversity Scholarship application — https://learn-more.scholarsapply.org/henkeldiversity/	**9** Entry due for Davidson Fellows Scholarship application process — http://www.davidsongifted.org/Fellows-Scholarship (OPEN TO ALL STUDENTS UNDER AGE 18) ***Deadline for Beinecke Scholarship nomination — http://fdnweb.org/beinecke/	**10** +Check website for International Bridge, Tunnel and Turnpike Association Scholarship Program application — https://www.ibtta.org/ibtta-foundation-scholarship-program	**11**	**12** Check website for Horatio Alger Career & Technical Scholarship Program Application — www.horatioalger.org or https://scholars.horatioalger.org
13 Simon Youth Foundation Scholarship application due soon — https://syf.org/scholarships/ Also see https://www.facebook.com/simonyouthfoundation or https://twitter.com/simon_youth	**14** Toshiba NSTA ExploraVision Awards application due this month— www.exploravision.org (OPEN TO STUDENTS IN GRADES K—12)	**15** Doodle 4 Google entry due soon — www.google.com/doodle4google (OPEN TO STUDENTS IN KINDERGARTEN THRU 12)	**16** Jeanette Rankin Women's Scholarship Fund application due soon — www.rankinfoundation.org (OPEN TO WOMEN 35 AND UP)	**17** Amazon Future Engineer Scholarship application due — https://learn-more.scholarsapply.org/amazonfutureengineer/	**18** Scholarships for Military Children application due — https://militaryscholar.org or https://fisherhouse.org/programs/scholarship-programs	**19** *Check website for Central Intelligence Agency (CIA) Undergraduate Scholarship Program application — https://www.cia.gov/careers/jobs/undergraduate-scholarship-program/
20 ***Check website for Central Intelligence Agency (CIA) Graduate Studies Scholarship Program application — https://www.cia.gov/careers/jobs/graduate-scholarship-program/	**21** **Check website— National Association for Campus Activities for scholarship opportunities - https://www.naca.org/FOUNDATION/Pages/Scholarships.aspx	**22** *+Check website for OppU Achievers Scholarship — https://www.opploans.com/scholarship	**23** Check website for Super Power Scholarship — https://www.unigo.com/scholarships/our-scholarships/superpower-scholarship (OPEN TO STUDENTS AGE 13 AND UP)	**24** *Check website for Bristol-Myers Squibb Scholarship for Cancer Survivors — https://learn-more.scholarsapply.org/cancer-survivors/ (OPEN TO STUDENTS 25 YEARS OLD OR YOUNGER)	**25**	**26**
27 Sweet and Simple Scholarship application due FEBRUARY 28 — https://www.unigo.com/scholarships/our-scholarships/sweet-and-simple-scholarship (OPEN TO STUDENTS AGE 13 AND UP)	**28** Life Lessons Essay and Video Contest application due MARCH 1 — www.lifehappens.org/life-lessons (FOR STUDENTS WHO HAVE BEEN AFFECTED BY THE DEATH OF A PARENT OR GUARDIAN)					

The Scholarship Monthly Planner

Notes

_____

_____

_____

_____

_____

_____

_____

_____

_____

_____

_____

_____

_____

_____

_____

_____

_____

_____

_____

_____

_____

_____

_____

DON'T FORGET!

- Final deadline dates have red text.
- Submit your application at least 7 days before the deadline.
- Always look at least 1 month ahead to get prepared for upcoming deadlines.
- Hate writing? Start on your essay at least 1 month prior to the deadline.
- Need recommendations? Ask at least 4 weeks prior to the deadline. Follow-up! Also, many programs request recommendations electronically. Please let someone know you've provided their e-mail address for a recommendation, so they will be prepared for the e-mail request.
- As you download applications, organize them. You should have one folder for each month. Place applications in the appropriate folder for each month. For example, all applications that are due in December should be in a folder marked December.
- Check previous months for application download dates or activities you need to complete. These activities are shown in black text. Although you may be behind with some activities, the deadline date for a scholarship or award may not have passed.
- Research and include local, regional, and state based scholarships in your calendar.
- Research and include scholarships based on your interests, personal characteristics, and situation in your calendar.
- Request nominations with a letter and your résumé.

The Scholarship Monthly Planner
March 2022

*Programs are open to current college students and high school seniors.

**Programs are open to current college students only.

***Programs are open to graduate and/or professional school students only.

+Program open to graduate and undergraduate students

Unless otherwise noted, all other programs are open to high school seniors.

SUN	MON	TUE	WED	THU	FRI	SAT
		1 *Leading the Future II Scholarship application due — www.scholarshipworkshop.com	**2** *Create-A-Greeting-Card Scholarship Contest entry due — www.gallerycollection.com/ greetingcardscontests.htm (OPEN TO NONTRADITIONAL and INTERNATIONAL STUDENTS)	**3** *Check website for Scorpion Cares Scholarship Program application — https://learnmore.scholarsapply.org/scorpion/	**4** Check for various Ayn Rand Essay Contest deadlines — www.aynrand.org or www.aynrand.org/students/essay-contests (Open to 8th grade high school students, college students, and adult students)	**5** Begin looking for local scholarship and award opportunities. Many may have deadlines in this month or later. To learn more about finding local opportunities, see the chapter, "The Local Scholarship Search: Finding Scholarships in Your Backyard" in *Winning Scholarships for College*, 5th edition.
6 *Check website for Varicent EDGE Scholarship application — https://learnmore.scholarsapply.org/varicentedge/ or https://www.varicent.com/company/edge-scholarship	**7** Begin working on Ayn Rand "The Fountainhead" Essay Contest entry — www.aynrand.org (OPEN TO 11TH AND 12TH GRADE HIGH SCHOOL STUDENTS)	**8** *Check website for Shawn Carter Scholarship — www.shawncartersf.com	**9** Check website for Ruth Lilly and Dorothy Sargent Rosenberg Poetry Fellowships— www.poetryfoundation.org/foundation/prizes_fellowship (OPEN TO NONTRADITIONAL STUDENTS)	**10** Check website for David Pruitt Award for Courage — https://learnmore.scholarsapply.org/courage/	**11**	**12** "Frame My Future" Scholarship Contest deadline soon — www.framemyfuture.com or https://www.diplomaframe.com/contests/frame-my-future-scholarship.aspx
13	**14** Check website for All About Education Scholarship — https://www.unigo.com/scholarships/our-scholarships/all-about-education-scholarship (OPEN TO STUDENTS AGE 13 AND UP)	**15** Horatio Alger Scholarship Application due — www.horatioalger.org or https://scholars.horatioalger.org	**16** Lockheed Martin Vocational Scholarship application due MARCH 17 — https://lockheedmartin.com/en-us/who-we-are/communities/stem-education/lockheed-martin-vocational-scholarship.html (OPEN TO STUDENTS PURSUING ASSOCIATE DEGREES OR CERTIFICATIONS)	**17** Henkel Diversity Scholarship application due — https://learnmore.scholarsapply.org/henkeldiversity/	**18** Check website for BHW Women in STEM Scholarship application—https://thebhwgroup.com/scholarship (ALSO OPEN TO INTERNATIONAL STUDENTS)	**19**
20 American Foreign Service Essay Contest entry due soon — www.afsa.org/essaycontest	**21**	**22** Jack Kent Cooke Young Scholars Program application due this month — www.jkcf.org/scholarships (OPEN TO 7TH GRADE STUDENTS ONLY)	**23**	**24**	**25**	**26**
27	**28** Start working on your outfit for the Stuck at Prom Contest — www.stuckatprom.com	**29** Super Power Scholarship deadline MARCH 31 — https://www.unigo.com/scholarships/our-scholarships/superpower-scholarship (OPEN TO STUDENTS AGE 13 AND UP)	**30** *+OppU Achievers Scholarship deadline MARCH 31 — https://www.opploans.com/scholarship	**31** *Orphan Foundation of America Foster Care to Success scholarship application due — http://fc2success.org		

The Scholarship Monthly Planner

Notes

_____
_____
_____
_____
_____
_____
_____
_____
_____
_____
_____
_____
_____
_____
_____
_____
_____
_____
_____
_____
_____
_____
_____
_____

DON'T FORGET!

- Final deadline dates have red text.
- Submit your application at least 7 days before the deadline.
- Always look at least 1 month ahead to get prepared for upcoming deadlines.
- Hate writing? Start on your essay at least 1 month prior to the deadline.
- Need recommendations? Ask at least 4 weeks prior to the deadline. Follow-up! Also, many programs request recommendations electronically. Please let someone know you've provided their e-mail address for a recommendation, so they will be prepared for the e-mail request.
- As you download applications, organize them. You should have one folder for each month. Place applications in the appropriate folder for each month. For example, all applications that are due in December should be in a folder marked December.
- Check previous months for application download dates or activities you need to complete. These activities are shown in black text. Although you may be behind with some activities, the deadline date for a scholarship or award may not have passed.
- Research and include local, regional, and state based scholarships in your calendar.
- Research and include scholarships based on your interests, personal characteristics, and situation in your calendar.
- Request nominations with a letter and your résumé.

The Scholarship Monthly Planner

April 2022

*Programs are open to current college students **and** high school seniors.

**Programs are open to current college students only.

***Programs are open to graduate and/or professional school students only.

+Program open to graduate and undergraduate students

Unless otherwise noted, all other programs are open to high school seniors.

SUN	MON	TUE	WED	THU	FRI	SAT
			If you haven't already, begin intensive research for community and state based scholarships and awards. Consider reading *Last Minute Guide to College Financing*.	*Lockheed Martin STEM Scholarship application due APRIL 1 — www.lockheedmartin.com/scholarship	**1** American Fire Sprinkler Association High School Senior Scholarship entry due — www.afsascholarship.org Also see @afsascholarship and www.facebook.com/afsascholarship/	**2** *Check website for Central Intelligence Agency (CIA) Undergraduate Scholarship Program application — https://www.cia.gov/careers/jobs/undergraduate-scholarship-program/
3 Check website for Kia Great Unknowns Scholarship application — https://learn-more.scholarsapply.org/kia/ (APPLY EARLY—ONLY FIRST 500 APPLICATIONS ACCEPTED)	**4** Varicent EDGE Scholarship application due — https://learn-more.scholarsapply.org/varicentedge/ or https://www.varicent.com/company/edge-scholarship	**5** *Check website for Shawn Carter Scholarship — www.shawncartersf.com	**6** David Pruitt Award for Courage application due APRIL 7 — https://learn-more.scholarsapply.org/courage/	**7** * Bristol-Myers Squibb Scholarship for Cancer Survivors application due— https://learn-more.scholarsapply.org/cancer-survivors/ (OPEN TO STUDENTS 25 YEARS OLD OR YOUNGER)	**8** ***Check website for Central Intelligence Agency (CIA) Graduate Scholarship Program application — https://https://www.cia.gov/careers/jobs/graduate-scholarship-program/	**9** Check website for Do-Over Scholarship — https://www.unigo.com/scholarships/our-scholarships/do-over-scholarship (OPEN TO STUDENTS AGE 13 AND UP)
10 Start working on your outfit for the Stuck at Prom Contest — www.stuckatprom.com Check website for Fifth Month Scholarship application — www.unigo.com/scholarships/our-scholarships/fifth-month-scholarship	**11** *Scorpion Cares Scholarship Program application due — https://learn-more.scholarsapply.org/scorpion/	**12** BHW Women in STEM Scholarship application due APRIL 15 — https://thebhwgroup.com/scholarship	**13** Gloria Barron Prize for Young Heroes application due APRIL 15— https://barronprize.org/apply (OPEN TO STUDENTS AGE 8 TO 18)	**14** +Alpha Kappa Alpha Educational Advancement Scholarship applications due, APRIL 15 — www.akaeaf.org	**15** Stockholm Junior Water Prize state competition entries due — www.wef.org/SJWP/ (OPEN TO GRADES 9 THRU 12)	**16** Check website for Navisite's Next Steminist Scholarship Program — https://www.navisite.com/navisites-next-steminist/ (OPEN TO FEMALES 25 OR YOUNGER PURSUING STEM MAJORS)
17 Check website for Cameron Impact Scholarship — https://www.bryancameroneducationfoundation.org	**18** +International Bridge, Tunnel and Turnpike Association Scholarship Program application due — https://www.ibtta.org/ibtta-foundation-scholarship-program	**19** *+ Check website for OppU Achievers Scholarship — https://www.opploans.com/scholarship	**20** Check website for Horatio Alger Career & Technical Scholarship Program Application — www.horatioalger.org or https://scholars.horatioalger.org	**21** *Check website for Workday Value Inclusion, Belonging and Equity (VIBE™) Scholarship — https://learn-more.scholarsapply.org/workday/	**22** Check website for College Express Scholarship Contest entry — https://www.collegexpress.com/carnegie_scholarship	**23**
24 Kia Great Unknowns Scholarship application due APRIL 29 — https://learn-more.scholarsapply.org/kia/ (APPLY EARLY—ONLY FIRST 500 APPLICATIONS ACCEPTED)	**25** Submission deadline for Ruth Lilly and Dorothy Sargent Rosenberg Poetry Fellowships deadline APRIL 30) — www.poetryfoundation.org/foundation/prizes_fellowship (OPEN TO NONTRADITIONAL STUDENTS)	**26** All About Education Scholarship application due APRIL 30 — https://www.unigo.com/scholarships/our-scholarships/all-about-education-scholarship (OPEN TO STUDENTS AGE 13 AND UP)	**27** Ayn Rand "Anthem" Essay Contest entries due APRIL 28 — www.aynrand.org (OPEN TO GRADES 8 THRU 10) ALSO OPEN TO INTERNATIONAL STUDENTS)	**28** Ayn Rand "The Fountainhead" Essay Contest entries due soon — www.aynrand.org (OPEN TO 11TH AND 12TH GRADE HIGH SCHOOL STUDENTS AND INTERNATIONAL STUDENTS)	**29** *Shawn Carter Scholarship application due APRIL 30 — www.shawncartersf.com Also see www.facebook.com/SCScholarship and www.twitter.com/ShawnCarterSF	**30** *+Ragins/Braswell National Scholarship application due — www.scholarshipworkshop.com

The Scholarship Monthly Planner

Notes

_____

_____

_____

_____

_____

_____

_____

_____

_____

_____

_____

_____

_____

_____

_____

_____

_____

_____

_____

_____

_____

_____

_____

_____

_____

DON'T FORGET!

- Final deadline dates have red text.
- Submit your application at least 7 days before the deadline.
- Always look at least 1 month ahead to get prepared for upcoming deadlines.
- Hate writing? Start on your essay at least 1 month prior to the deadline.
- Need recommendations? Ask at least 4 weeks prior to the deadline. Follow-up! Also, many programs request recommendations electronically. Please let someone know you've provided their e-mail address for a recommendation, so they will be prepared for the e-mail request.
- As you download applications, organize them. You should have one folder for each month. Place applications in the appropriate folder for each month. For example, all applications that are due in December should be in a folder marked December.
- Check previous months for application download dates or activities you need to complete. These activities are shown in black text. Although you may be behind with some activities, the deadline date for a scholarship or award may not have passed.
- Research and include local, regional, and state based scholarships in your calendar.
- Research and include scholarships based on your interests, personal characteristics, and situation in your calendar.
- Request nominations with a letter and your résumé.

The Scholarship Monthly Planner
May 2022

*Programs are open to current college students and high school seniors.

**Programs are open to current college students only.

***Programs are open to graduate and/or professional school students only.

+Program open to graduate and undergraduate students

Unless otherwise noted, all other programs are open to high school seniors.

SUN	MON	TUE	WED	THU	FRI	SAT
1 *+Dr. Angela E. Grant Memorial Scholarship deadline — http://drangelagrantscholarship.org (OPEN TO CANCER SURVIVORS OR THOSE WITH IMMEDIATE FAMILY MEMBERS DIAGNOSED WITH CANCER)	**2** **RISE Financial Progress Scholarship application due — https://www.risecredit.com/rise-scholarship	**3** **Check website for application: Tylenol Future Care Scholarship Program — www.tylenol.com/news/subptyschol	**4** *Check website for "One Planet, Many People" Video Contest entry — https://www.populationmedia.org/about-us/video-contest (ALSO OPEN TO INTERNATIONAL STUDENTS)	**5**	**6**	**7**
8	**9** **Check website for Americanism Educational Leaders Essay Contest — https://infoguides.pepperdine.edu/AEL	**10**	**11**	**12**	**13**	**14**
15	**16** Navisite's Next Steminist Scholarship application due — https://www.navisite.com/navisites-next-steminist/ (OPEN TO FEMALES 25 OR YOUNGER PURSUING STEM MAJORS)	**17** Workday Value Inclusion, Belonging and Equity (VIBE™) Scholarship application due — https://learn-more.scholarsapply.org/workday/	**18** *+DoSomething.org Easy Scholarships deadlines soon — https://www.dosomething.org/us/about/easy-scholarships or www.dosomething.org (see Scholarships) This site has various scholarships with deadlines usually at the end of the month.	**19**	**20**	**21**
22	**23**	**24** *+ Check website for OppU Achievers Scholarship — https://www.opploans.com/scholarship	**25** +Complete Military Spouse Scholarship application (awards made quarterly)— www.militaryfamily.org or https://www.militaryfamily.org/programs/spouses-scholarships/ (OPEN TO NONTRADITIONAL STUDENTS)	**26**	**27**	**28**
29 College Express Scholarship Contest entry deadline — https://www.collegexpress.com/carnegie_scholarship	**30**	**31** Fifth Month Scholarship application due — www.unigo.com/scholarships/our-scholarships/fifth-month-scholarship				

The Scholarship Monthly Planner

Notes

_____

The Scholarship Monthly Planner
June 2022

*Programs are open to current college students and high school seniors.

**Programs are open to current college students only.

***Programs are open to graduate and/or professional school students only.

+Program open to graduate and undergraduate students

Unless otherwise noted, all other programs are open to high school seniors.

SUN	MON	TUE	WED	THU	FRI	SAT
			1 **Begin work on Platt Family Scholarship Prize Essay Contest entry — www.thelincolnforum.org/scholarship-essay-contest (OPEN TO FULL-TIME, UNDERGRADUATE STUDENTS IN AN AMERICAN COLLEGE OR UNIVERSITY. US CITIZENSHIP IS NOT REQUIRED.)	**2** Tylenol Future Care Scholarship Program application due this month — www.tylenol.com/news/subptyschol)	**3** Stuck at Prom Contest entries due this month — www.stuckatprom.com Check website for official rules.	**4**
5	**6**	**7** **Check website— National Association for Campus Activities for scholarship opportunities - https://www.naca.org/FOUNDATION/Pages/Scholarships.aspx	**8**	**9**	**10**	**11**
12	**13**	**14** Check website for Horatio Alger Career & Technical Scholarship Program Application — www.horatioalger.org or https://scholars.horatioalger.org	**15**	**16**	**17** *Central Intelligence Agency (CIA) Undergraduate Scholarship Program application due JUNE 18 — https://www.cia.gov/careers/jobs/undergraduate-scholarship-program/	**18** ***Central Intelligence Agency (CIA) Graduate Studies Scholarship Program application due — https://www.cia.gov/careers/jobs/graduate-scholarship-program/
19	**20**	**21**	**22**	**23** +DoSomething.org Easy Scholarships deadlines soon — https://www.dosomething.org/us/about/easy-scholarships or www.dosomething.org *(see Scholarships)* This site has various scholarships with deadlines usually at the end of the month.	**24**	**25**
26	**27** Americanism Educational Leaders Essay Contest submission due JUNE 30 — https://infoguides.pepperdine.edu/AEL	**28** Do-Over Scholarship deadline JUNE 30 — https://www.unigo.com/scholarships/our-scholarships/do-over-scholarship (OPEN TO STUDENTS AGE 13 AND UP)	**29** *+OppU Achievers Scholarship deadline JUNE 30 — https://www.opploans.com/scholarship	**30** *Have a disability? Wells Fargo Scholarship Program for People with Disabilities application due — https://learnmore.scholarsapply.org/pwdscholarship/ (Apply early. They have a strict application limit.)		

The Scholarship Monthly Planner

Notes

_____

_____

_____

_____

_____

_____

_____

_____

_____

_____

_____

_____

_____

_____

_____

_____

_____

_____

_____

_____

_____

_____

_____

_____

_____

DON'T FORGET!

- Final deadline dates have red text.
- Submit your application at least 7 days before the deadline.
- Always look at least 1 month ahead to get prepared for upcoming deadlines.
- Hate writing? Start on your essay at least 1 month prior to the deadline.
- Need recommendations? Ask at least 4 weeks prior to the deadline. Follow-up! Also, many programs request recommendations electronically. Please let someone know you've provided their e-mail address for a recommendation, so they will be prepared for the e-mail request.
- As you download applications, organize them. You should have one folder for each month. Place applications in the appropriate folder for each month. For example, all applications that are due in December should be in a folder marked December.
- Check previous months for application download dates or activities you need to complete. These activities are shown in black text. Although you may be behind with some activities, the deadline date for a scholarship or award may not have passed.
- Research and include local, regional, and state based scholarships in your calendar.
- Research and include scholarships based on your interests, personal characteristics, and situation in your calendar.
- Request nominations with a letter and your résumé.

The Scholarship Monthly Planner

July 2022

*Programs are open to current college students <u>and</u> high school seniors.

**Programs are open to current college students only.

***Programs are open to graduate and/or professional school students only.

+Program open to graduate and undergraduate students

Unless otherwise noted, all other programs are open to high school seniors.

SUN	MON	TUE	WED	THU	FRI	SAT
				If you will be a college freshman in the upcoming academic year, get ready now for upcoming August deadlines and activities.	**1** **Wells Fargo Veterans Scholarship program application due — https://learn-more.scholarsapply.org/wellsfargoveterans/	**2** Current college students should research associations and organizations related to their major or minor for scholarship and award opportunities.
3	**4**	**5** *+Check website for DoSomething.org Easy Scholarships — https://www.dosomething.org/us/about/easy-scholarships or www.dosomething.org *(see Scholarships)*	**6** **Check website for Optimal Scholarships — https://www.optimal.com/scholarships	**7**	**8**	**9**
10	**11** Graduate and professional school students should research government agencies and research oriented companies in need of individuals from their study area.	**12**	**13**	**14** "One Planet, Many People" Video Contest entry due JULY 15 — https://www.populationmedia.org/about-us/video-contest (ALSO OPEN TO INTERNATIONAL STUDENTS)	**15** Horatio Alger Career & Technical Scholarship Program Application due — https://scholars.horatioalger.org/about-our-scholarship-programs/technical/ (THIS IS A PRIORITY DEADLINE. YOU MAY BE ABLE TO SUBMIT AFTER THIS DATE)	**16**
17	**18**	**19**	**20**	**21**	**22**	**23**
24	**25** +DoSomething.org Easy Scholarships deadlines soon — https://www.dosomething.org/us/about/easy-scholarships or www.dosomething.org *(see Scholarships)* This site has various scholarships with deadlines usually at the end of the month.	**26**	**27** *	**28**	**29**	**30**
31 **Platt Family Scholarship Prize Essay Contest entry due JULY 31 — www.thelincolnforum.org/scholarship-essay-contest (OPEN TO FULL-TIME, UNDERGRADUATE STUDENTS IN AN AMERICAN COLLEGE OR UNIVERSITY. US CITIZENSHIP IS NOT REQUIRED.)						

The Scholarship Monthly Planner

Notes

_____

_____

_____

_____

_____

_____

_____

_____

_____

_____

_____

_____

_____

_____

_____

_____

_____

_____

_____

_____

_____

DON'T FORGET!

- Final deadline dates have red text.
- Submit your application at least 7 days before the deadline.
- Always look at least 1 month ahead to get prepared for upcoming deadlines.
- Hate writing? Start on your essay at least 1 month prior to the deadline.
- Need recommendations? Ask at least 4 weeks prior to the deadline. Follow-up! Also, many programs request recommendations electronically. Please let someone know you've provided their e-mail address for a recommendation, so they will be prepared for the e-mail request.
- As you download applications, organize them. You should have one folder for each month. Place applications in the appropriate folder for each month. For example, all applications that are due in December should be in a folder marked December.
- Check previous months for application download dates or activities you need to complete. These activities are shown in black text. Although you may be behind with some activities, the deadline date for a scholarship or award may not have passed.
- Research and include local, regional, and state based scholarships in your calendar.
- Research and include scholarships based on your interests, personal characteristics, and situation in your calendar.
- Request nominations with a letter and your résumé.

The Scholarship Monthly Planner

Important Notes & Reminders

- The scholarship programs and awards shown in *The Scholarship Monthly Planner* may not represent all scholarships available to you. Those listed are generally available to a majority of students. Please conduct additional research to find scholarships in your community and state as well as those that apply to your situation and specific interests. To learn how to find additional scholarships, read *Winning Scholarships for College* or attend a workshop or online class conducted by Marianne Ragins. You can also visit www.scholarshipworkshop.com and refer to the scholarship search or scholarship help section as well as the books and resources section for more information about online searches.

- Deadline dates may have changed prior to or after the publication of *The Scholarship Monthly Planner*. Please use the information provided to check the most current deadline date. In some cases, the prior year's date may be included to give an approximate timeframe for the current year's deadline. *COVID-19 may also alter deadlines or the availability of a scholarship, award, or prize.*

- Scholarship and award programs may be discontinued at any time.

- Some programs and awards included in the planner require nominations before you can submit an application. Use the contact information to find out to how to be nominated for a scholarship or award. For more information on requesting nominations, read *Winning Scholarships for College,* which includes a nomination request letter and other information.

- Some dates in the planner list more than one scholarship or award program.

- All text in red indicates a scholarship or award deadline. Space does not allow indication of whether this is a postmark or receipt date. To ensure your application or entry is received within the appropriate timeframe, please visit the website shown for more information and submit your application at least 7 days prior to the date shown in the calendar.

The Scholarship Workshop LLC and Marianne Ragins have no control over the quality, safety or legality of the scholarships or awards shown nor the ability of the scholarship and award sponsors/providers to provide scholarships or awards. *The Scholarship Monthly Planner* may contain inaccuracies or typographical errors. The Scholarship Workshop LLC nor Marianne Ragins make no representations concerning the accuracy, reliability, completeness, or timeliness of any information included in *The Scholarship Monthly Planner*. The use of *The Scholarship Monthly Planner* is at your own risk. Changes are periodically made to *The Scholarship Monthly Planner* and may be made at any time.